MY FIRST BOOK

BRAZIL

ALL ABOUT BRAZIL FOR KIDS

GLOBED
CHILDREN BOOKS

Interior and cover Design: Daniel Day
Editor: Margaret Bam

For My Sons, Daniel, David and Jude

Christ The Redeemer

Brazil

Brazil is a **country**.

A country is land that is controlled by a **single government**. Countries are also called **nations, states, or nation-states**.

Countries can be **different sizes**. Some countries are big and others are small.

Rio de Janeiro, Brazil

Where Is Brazil?

Brazil is located in the continent of South America.

A continent is a massive area of land that is separated from others by water or other natural features.

Brazil is situated in the eastern part of South America.

Brasilia cityscape, Brazil

Capital

The capital of Brazil is Brasília.

Brasília is located in the **central west region** of the country.

São Paulo is the largest city in Brazil.

Sugarloaf Mountain, Rio de Janeiro, Brazil

States

Brazil is a country that is made up of 26 states

The states of Brazil are as follows:

Acre, Alagoas, Amapa, Amazonas, Bahia, Ceara, Distrito Federal, Espirito Santo, Goias, Maranhao, Mato Grosso, Mato Grosso do Sul, Minas Gerais, Para, Paraiba, Parana, Pernambuco, Piaui, Rio de Janeiro, Rio Grande do Norte, Rio Grande do Sul, Rondonia, Roraima, Santa Catarina, Sao Paulo, Sergipe and Tocantins.

Traditional drummers in Salvador, Brazil

Population

Brazil has population of around **217 million people** making it the 7th most populated country in the world and the most populated country in South America.

Sao Luis, Maranhao State, Brazil

Size

Brazil is **8,515,767 square kilometres** making it the largest country in South America by area.

Brazil is the 5th largest country in the world.

Languages

The official language of Brazil is Portuguese. The Portuguese language is spoken by hundreds of millions of people across the world.

Brazil is the only Portuguese-speaking nation in the Americas

Here are a few Portuguese phrases
- **Bom día-** Good morning
- **Tudo bem? -** Everything well?
- **Obrigado** - Thank you

Brasilia Cathedral, Brasilia, Brazil

Attractions

There are lots of interesting places to see in Brazil.

Some beautiful places to visit in Brazil are

- **Christ the Redeemer**
- **Ibirapuera Park**
- **Escadaria Selarón**
- **Iguazu Falls**
- **Cathedral of Brasília**
- **Sugarloaf Mountain**

Salvador, Brazil

History of Brazil

People have lived in Brazil for a very long time, in fact it is believed that humans have inhabited Brazil as far back as 11,000 years ago.

Brazil was claimed by the Portuguese Empire on 22 April 1500, with the arrival of the Portuguese fleet commanded by Pedro Álvares Cabral.

Brazil gained independence from Portugal on 7 September 1822.

Copacabana Beach, Rio de Janeiro, Brazil

Customs in Brazil

Brazil has many fascinating customs and traditions.

- Brazil is home to the biggest carnival in the world called The Rio Carnival. Each year around 2 million people take to the streets to enjoy dancing, music and parades in incredible carnival outfits.
- On September 26th and 27th, The Day of Patron Saint Cosme and Patron Saint Damian is celebrated. On these days, it is a customary to hand out sweets and toys to children who spend the day on the streets.

Music of Brazil

There are many different music genres in Brazil such as **Samba, Música popular brasileira, Bossa nova, Funk carioca, Axé, Música sertaneja, Choro and Forró.**

Some notable Brazilian musicians include
- **Antônio Carlos Jobim**
- **João Gilberto**
- **Gilberto Gil**
- **Claudia Leitte**
- **Roberto Carlos**
- **MV Bill**
- **Elba Ramalho**

Feijoada

Food of Brazil

Brazil is known for having delicious, flavoursome and rich dishes.

The national dish of Brazil is **Feijoada** which is a delicious and hearty stew dish made with beans and pork. Feijoada is often served with farofa, toasted cassava flour.

Food of Brazil

Some popular dishes in Brazil include

- **Moqueca de Camarão.**
- **Vatapá**
- **Acarajé**
- **Deep fried Pastel**
- **Empadão**
- **Bolinho de Bacalhau**
- **Moqueca**
- **Cachaça**

Estaiada Bridge, Sao Paulo, Brazil

Weather in Brazil

Brazil is a very big country and its weather varies considerably from north to south. Most of Brazil has a **humid tropical and subtropical climate**. However some parts of the country, particularly the southern parts and mountains can experience milder weather.

Amazon Rainforest, Acre, Brazil

Animals of Brazil

There are many wonderful animals in Brazil.

Here are some animals that live in Brazil

- Toco toucan
- Anteater
- Three-toed sloth
- Piranha
- Capybara
- Armadillo
- Yacara caiman

Jericoacoara, Brazil

Beaches

There are many beautiful beaches in Brazil which is one of the reasons why so many people visit this beautiful country every year.

Here are some of Brazil's beaches

- Copacabana
- Ilha Grande
- Ipanema
- Buzios Resort Town
- Jericoacoara
- Florianopolis

People at Brazilian soccer game

Sports of Brazil

Sports play an integral part in Brazilian culture. The most popular sport is **Football.**

Here are some of famous sportspeople from Brazil

- **Pelé - Football**
- **Neymar - Football**
- **Joaquim Cruz - Athletics**
- **Anderson Varejão - Basketball**
- **Ronaldinho - Football**
- **Robinho - Football**

Person with Brazilian flag

Famous

Many successful people hail from Brazil.

Here are some notable Brazilian figures

- **Gisele Bündchen – Model**
- **Paulo Coelho – Novelist**
- **Adriana Lima – Model**
- **Rodrigo Santoro – Actor**
- **Morena Baccarin – Actress**

Caracol Falls, Brazil

Something Extra...

As a little something extra, we are going to share some lesser known facts about Brazil.

- **There more than 400 airports in Brazil.**
- **Brazil is the worlds largest exporter of coffee.**
- **Silva is the most popular name in Brazil.**

Words From the Author

We hope that you enjoyed learning about the wonderful country of Brazil.

Brazil is a country rich in culture and beauty, with lots of wonderful places to visit and people to meet.

We hope you continue to learn more about this wonderful nation. If you enjoyed this book, consider leaving a review!

With Love

Printed in Great Britain
by Amazon

40561176R00027